Sandro Natalini

What

Came

First?

Tundra Books

What
came first?
The chicken?
The egg?
The story began
long ago with . . .

carbon dioxide!

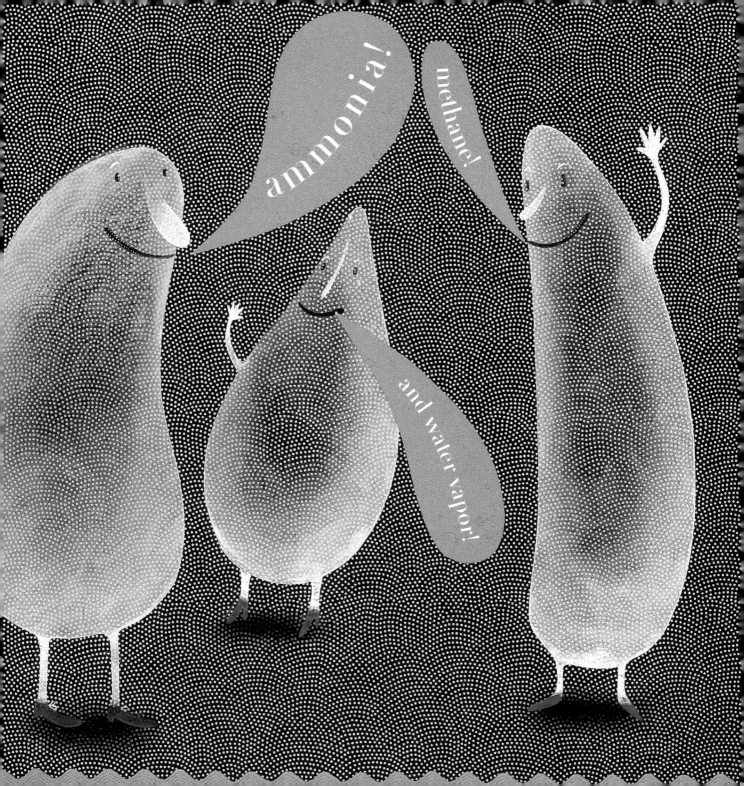

Who better to help answer the BIG QUESTION "*What came first?*" But you don't need to be **a chicken** to recognize an **egg.** You can learn about it too.

TABLE GRAPES RIBIER GRAPES
BAGGED NET WT. 21

JINDY

GROWERS-SHIPPERS JAKE J. CESARE & SONS DELANO

16

Lots of stories begin with "once upon a time," and so does this one; close to fourteen billion years ago, according to scientists.

Imagine a very small bubble, a blister with an interior that is dense and hot. Suddenly, the blister bursts and forms an enormous ball of burning rock. The explosion must have been enormous. In fact, scientists call it the

BIG BANG.

Was that how the universe was born, billions of years ago – the universe and the galaxies, the stars and the planets, including our own, and all the living things we know?

In time, the ball of rock began to cool. Scientists think that the steam from years of volcanic eruptions formed storm clouds loaded with rain. That rain formed enormous expanses of water – the first oceans.

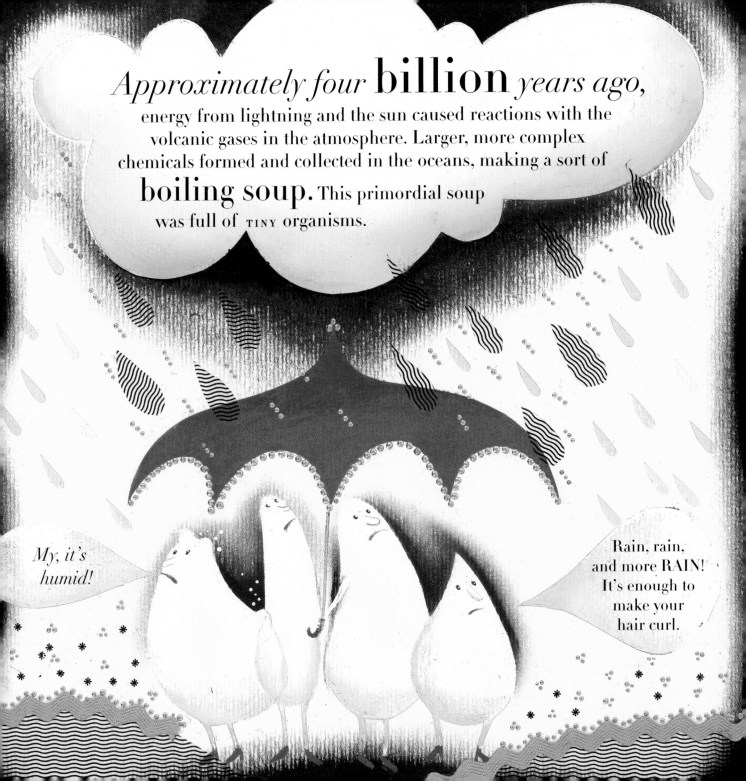

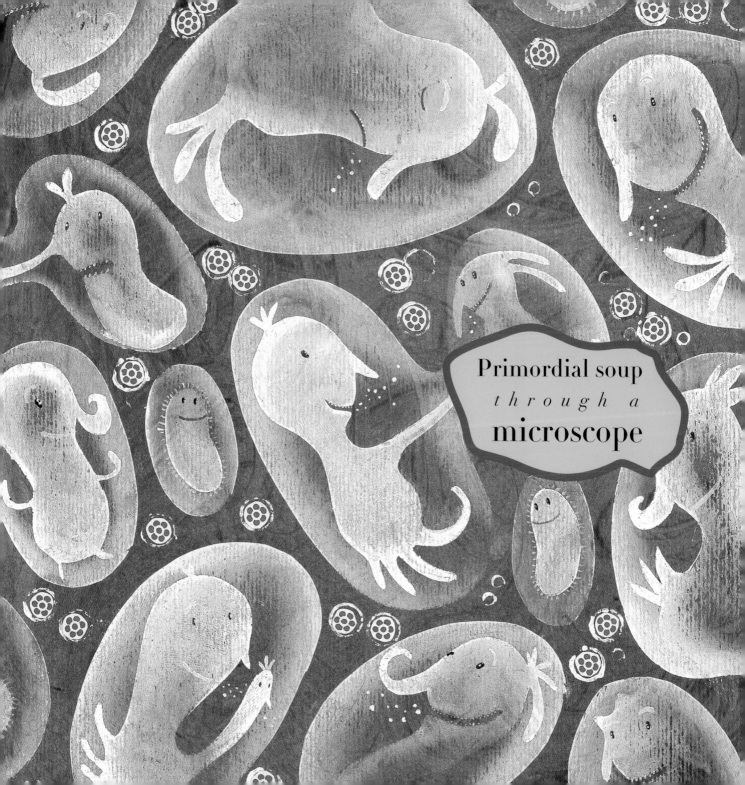

Primordial soup *through a* microscope

With the passage of time, the temperature in the oceans fell and more creatures formed: sponges, coral, and sea anemones, jellyfish and worms – the fantastic beginnings of life on Earth.

MEET SOME OF THE OLDEST of old-timers. The amoeba can change its shape. It can even split in two and clone itself. It feeds on algae and bacteria that are so tiny you can't see them without a microscope.

This paramecium is shaped like the sole of a shoe, and it's actually much smaller than an amoeba.

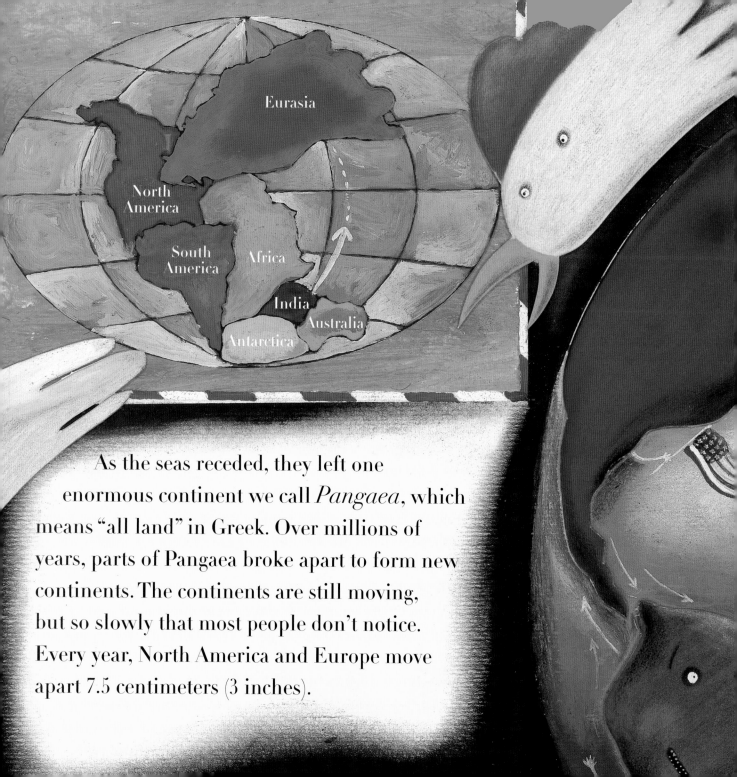

As the seas receded, they left one enormous continent we call *Pangaea*, which means "all land" in Greek. Over millions of years, parts of Pangaea broke apart to form new continents. The continents are still moving, but so slowly that most people don't notice. Every year, North America and Europe move apart 7.5 centimeters (3 inches).

The Paleozoic Era
543 – 248 million years ago

The waters teemed with creatures like jellyfish and mollusks. The first fish appeared, and so did starfish, squid, and gigantic polyps. Some sea creatures were tiny, but others were huge: marine scorpions over 2 meters (6.5 feet) long; fish as big as a truck, covered with a sort of armor; and the ancestors of sharks, 16 meters (52 feet) long. The first land plants appeared during this era and you would have seen mammal-like reptiles. By the end of the Paleozoic era, the ancestors of insects, able to live out of water for at least part of the time, began to form.

The Mesozoic Era
248 – 65 million years ago

In this era, thick and luxuriant vegetation began to cover the dry land. Some creatures that could live on land and in water began to lose their ability to survive in water. You would have recognized turtles, crocodiles, and lizards. But other creatures were like nothing alive today. Some were as small as a chicken; others were the size of a train. We call the meat eaters carnivores and the plant eaters herbivores, and we call the ones that ate both meat and plants omnivores.

This was the era of the (non-avian) dinosaurs. They first appeared about 230 million years ago. Birds, then true mammals appeared about 170 million years ago. Flowering plants appeared about 130 million years ago.

Tertiary Period

65 – 2 million years ago

In some areas, vast prairies slowly took the place of forests. The skies were full of birds, descendants of the dinosaurs. Some birds had small wings and didn't fly – they ran. The barylambda was about 2.5 meters (8 feet) long, with a short head and a strong tail like a kangaroo's. The tail might have been useful for leaning on while the barylambda munched on leaves. You would have seen shrews and the ancestors of horses, which were little larger than a dog and had four toes on the forefeet and three toes on the hind feet. True horses were around by the end of the Tertiary period.

Quaternary Period

2 million years ago to today

At the beginning of the period, when glaciers blanketed expanses of land, the ancestors of bears, rhinoceroses, mammoths, and tigers were covered in thick fur to protect them from the cold. But as the temperatures rose, it became harder for them to survive. Scientists have found individuals perfectly preserved, imprisoned in the ice. In some cases, they still had their heavy fur. And this is the age when human beings appeared.

WHY DID ALL THIS CHANGE HAPPEN, and why is it still happening? Why did one kind of plant or creature give way to another? Some scientists think that climate change – too much heat or cold – could make it difficult for creatures to find food and shelter. Other scientists believe that terrible volcanic eruptions covered the ground with lava,

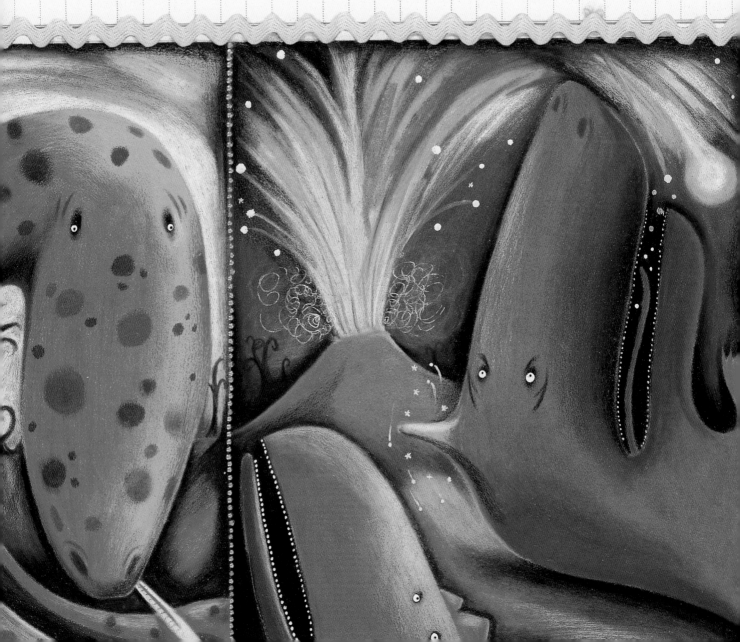

killing plants and animals alike. There are those who believe that an enormous meteorite may have hit the earth, setting off fires on land and tsunamis at sea.

What is certain is that Earth and the creatures on it are connected, and that living things have adapted in order to survive – a process we call EVOLUTION.

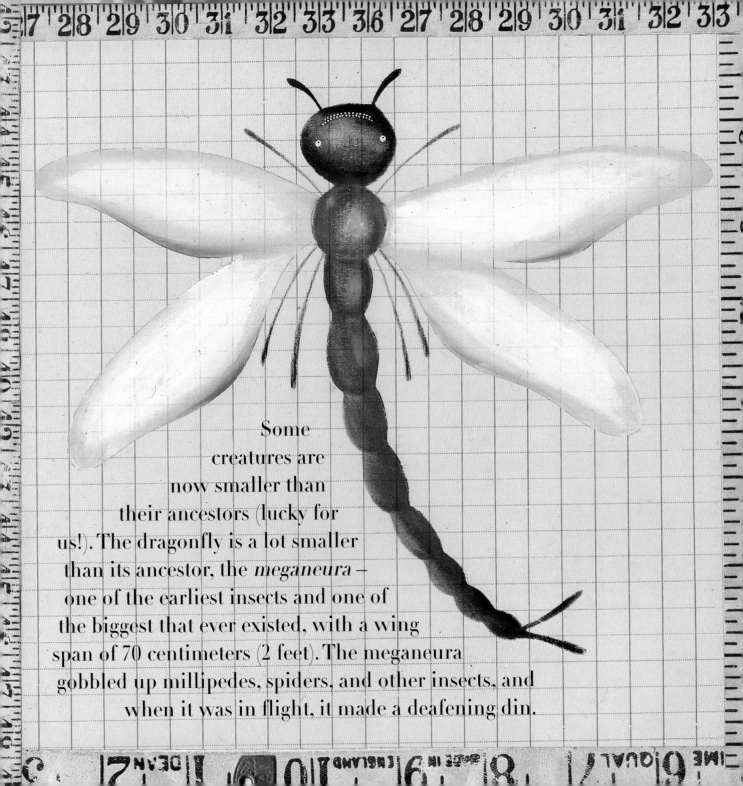

Some
creatures are
now smaller than
their ancestors (lucky for
us!). The dragonfly is a lot smaller
than its ancestor, the *meganeura* –
one of the earliest insects and one of
the biggest that ever existed, with a wing
span of 70 centimeters (2 feet). The meganeura
gobbled up millipedes, spiders, and other insects, and
when it was in flight, it made a deafening din.

We study why changes take place and why they don't. Why didn't tortoises, which are much the same now as they were millions of years ago, vanish when the dinosaurs did? Tortoises can live for a hundred years or more. **Maybe it's because they eat their veggies and take life easy.**

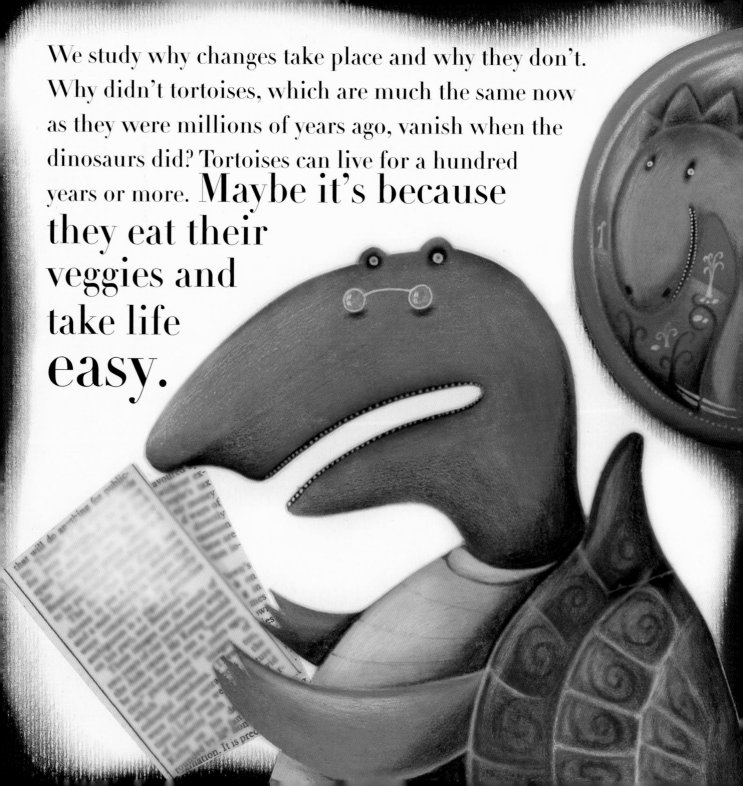

And if you were to go back to the Mesozoic era, you would recognize the crocodile's ancestors by their sharp teeth and strong jaws. Perhaps it was so well adapted to its environment that it hasn't had to change much.

We know all
this from studying
the bones and fossils
that all these creatures
left behind. That study is called
paleontology. Sir Richard Owen
(1804–1892) was a paleontologist
who coined the word *Dinosauria*.
With infinite patience, he
identified and rebuilt
fossilized bones
to assemble the
skeletons of
"fearfully great reptiles," which is what
DINOSAUR means.

Another kind of
historical record comes from
our own ancestors. In Spain,
Italy, France, Sweden, and Great
Britain, the earliest artists left a
record of hunting and rituals,
giving us a precious glimpse
into the distant past.

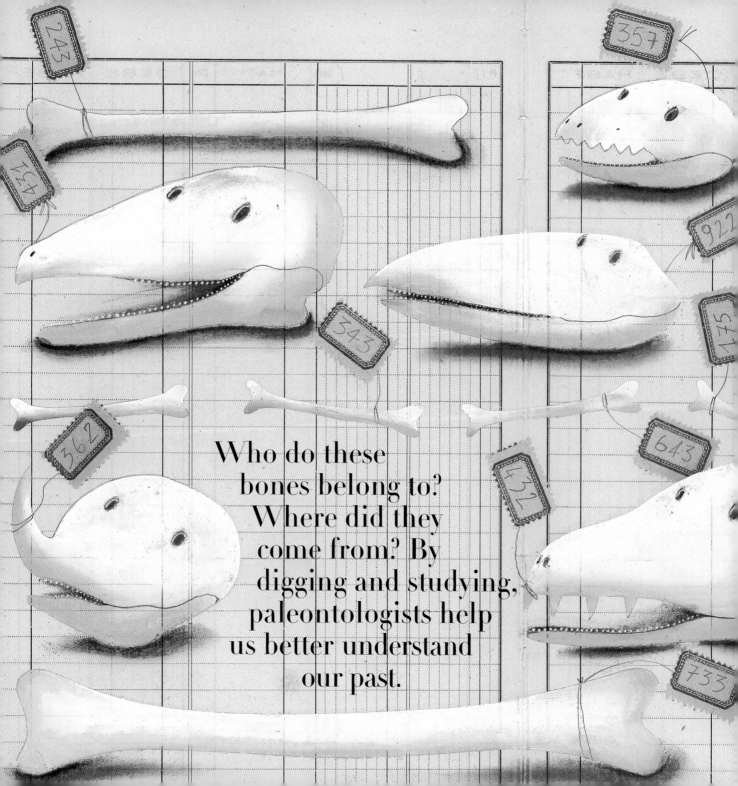

Who do these bones belong to? Where did they come from? By digging and studying, paleontologists help us better understand our past.

Extinction

can happen over millions of years, or it can be brutally quick. The dodo had existed for thousands of years until the 17th century. It had small wings that couldn't carry it, but it had few enemies. It was no match for human beings, though. It became one of the thousands of species that have become extinct during the time of human history.

Many species have

{ vanished }

in recent history, such as the
great auk, the passenger pigeon,
and the spectacled cormorant.

Charles Darwin wondered about what came first and what would cause life-forms to change. He studied all kinds of birds and animals, including monkeys and apes. He wondered whether we might have something in common with them – like a common ancestor. He wrote about how animals and plants adapt, and *we've been talking about evolution ever since.*

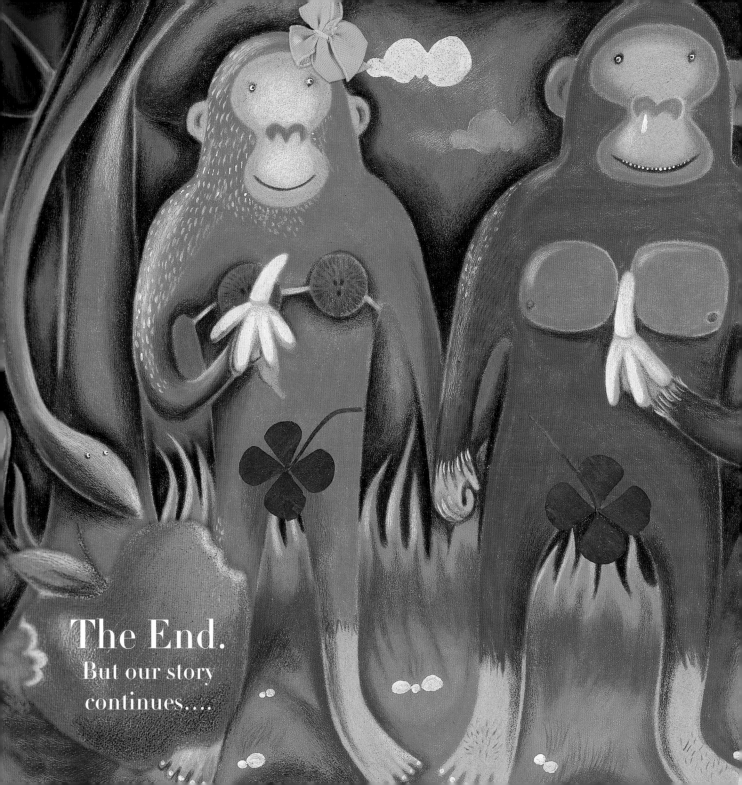

The End.
But our story
continues....

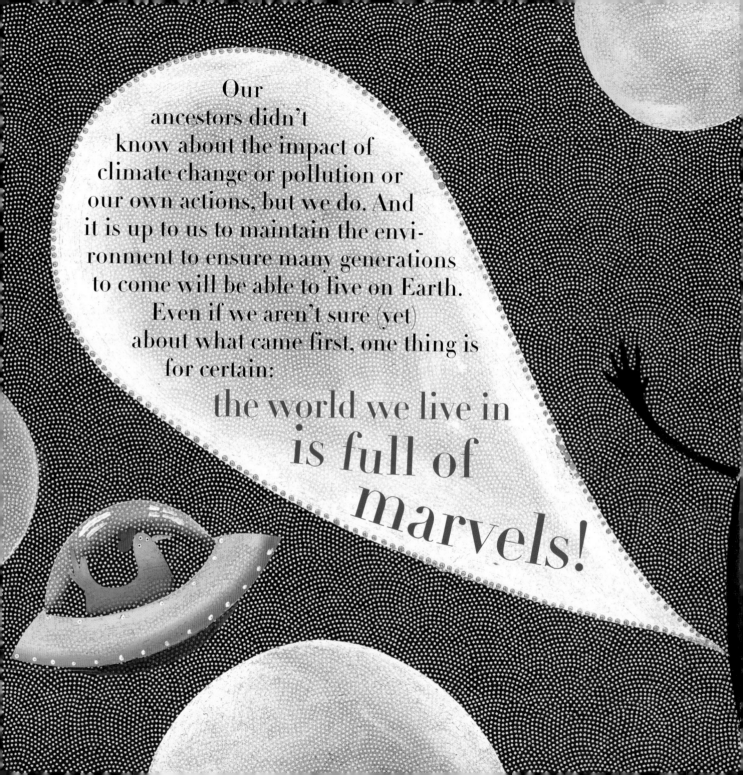

Our
ancestors didn't
know about the impact of
climate change or pollution or
our own actions, but we do. And
it is up to us to maintain the environment to ensure many generations
to come will be able to live on Earth.
Even if we aren't sure (yet)
about what came first, one thing is
for certain:

the world we live in
is full of
marvels!